Chase

Josephine

Paul

Megan

Daniela

Ally

Katie

Ruth

St. Didacus Parish School
Student Council
2011 - 2012

Suzanne

alexandra

Katherine

Claire

Mitchell

grace

Isaiah

Emma

PATRONS AND PROTECTORS

In Times of Need

Art and commentary by

Michael O'Neill McGrath, OSFS

Foreword by Rosemary Luling Haughton

LITURGY
TRAINING
PUBLICATIONS

acknowledgments

Dedicated with heart-filled gratitude to Father Joe Morrisey, Brother Bob Drelich and all my brothers in the Oblates of Saint Francis de Sales whose support guides me along.

PATRONS AND PROTECTORS: IN TIMES OF NEED © 2002 Archdiocese of Chicago: Liturgy Training Publications, 1800 North Hermitage Avenue, Chicago IL 60622-1101; 1-800-933-1800; fax 1-800-933-7094; orders@ltp.org; www.ltp.org. All rights reserved.

Visit our website at www.ltp.org.

This book was edited by Margaret M. Brennan. Audrey Novak Riley was the production editor. The design is by Anna Manhart, and the typesetting was done by Anne Fritzinger in Berkeley, Adobe Jenson and Mrs Eaves. Printed by Palace Press International in China.

Library of Congress Control Number: 2002116724

PPOC3

contents

foreword

The really hard experiences in our lives show us up. We thought we were safe and strong, that our lives were secure, our relationships, loving—and suddenly that floor of our lives seems to fall out from under us.

It is in such times of fear, uncertainty, loss that we find ourselves drawing on memories of how other people have dealt with difficult times. We remember examples of a beloved teacher or grandmother or friend. There are others, too—people we have never known but who are there for us, men and women and children—whose lives were changed by suffering and loss and grief but who were not defeated. Memories of them are preserved for us and can become our memories too—real memories of real friends.

When we are confronted with truly frightening, even dangerous, experiences, those memories can help us keep going, keep hoping, keep caring for other people in our lives. Perhaps we feel afraid, furious at God—we want to blame someone for what has happened. That's natural, and saints and heroes and heroines are not exempt from those feelings—but they and we don't get stuck in them. They and we can move on, and not just survive our troubles but become better, stronger, more compassionate than before.

The experiences that shake us to the core are not always those that affect us directly—our own loss or illness. We can be just as deeply shaken by bad things that happen to those we love, or by hearing of suffering or disaster even in distant places. In fact, we can feel greater outrage, pain, desperate grief, because of what is happening to others. Our helplessness is often the worst suffering—we can do so little to help.

Yet in this, too, the knowledge that others have faced the same pain and have found a way to go on, to transform the experience through love and compassion, gives us courage. We remember—not only people we have known directly but those like the people in this book, people whom we know in imagination, people who were and are real, people who have been in those terrible places and transformed them—and been transformed themselves.

Saints are an odd lot of people, some of them not at all what we would call "saintly." Among those we call saints are people who were narrow-minded or tiresome or self-righteous. They shared the prejudices of their time and class. Some had a wild and disastrous youth. We might not have enjoyed the real-life company of some of these saints at all!

What makes the difference in the end is the strange thing we call faith. None of us is born with it; sometimes it seems to emerge strongly in childhood; sometimes it comes late, and painfully. But faith seems to allow all the goodness someone is capable of to flourish so strongly that the person can live through even the hardest experiences with courage, even humor, even joy. Faith is so mysterious—it's an unfathomable happening between the person and God. Somehow the experience of pain and sorrow is what actually breaks down defenses and sets that person free.

Some of the people in this book we know a lot about; it's easy to imagine them, talk to them. Of some we know little, but they are shining symbols of qualities we can recognize and respond to. They are people who went through loss, fear, grief, pain—the kind of things that strip away defenses and leave the soul naked before God. So they are people we can cry out to, complain to, grumble to. One with God, they are one with our need and our hope. Their lives can release in us the faith we didn't know we had.

Rosemary Luling Haughton
Director of Wellspring
Gloucester, Massachusetts

Saint Agatha
patron of people with breast cancer

SAINT AGATHA, ONE OF THE MOST BELOVED EARLY CHRISTIAN martyrs, lived and died in Sicily in the third century. Like other Christians in the days of Roman persecution, Agatha suffered many tortures because of her faith. She was placed on a rack, rolled over hot coals and broken glass, and her breasts were cut off, which is why she is prayed to by those with breast cancer. Shortly before her death in prison, Agatha had a vision of Saint Peter, who encouraged her in her faith and brought her inner strength and consolation.

Agatha's jacket is red, the traditional color of martyrs, and her green tee-shirt is a symbol of healing and hope. It is said that throughout her agonies, Agatha remained peaceful and calm. Her last words, a prayer of gratitude, are in the border.

On her jacket is the popular symbol of the fight against breast cancer, a pink ribbon. Agatha runs to the finish line in a race for the cure, drawing our attention to the thousands of women who endure breast cancer and offering the same hope that Saint Peter gave to her. The message is clear: Hang in there, and if we stand together—or run together—we will see the struggle through to a victorious end.

Saint Agatha's feast is February 5.

Before August of 1982 I had never been ill, not even with the measles. Life had been good to me, even through my mother's death at age 47 of breast cancer. My mom's sister died at age 49 of the same disease, and I was told I was at greater risk. Still, I was not prepared.

Then at 42 I was diagnosed with breast cancer. I got through the treatment and breathed a sigh of relief. Five and a half years later, I had a second, much more serious, stage three primary breast cancer.

Within two years, my older sister was also diagnosed with cancer and we knew she would die. I searched my soul to find some peace. I was filled with rage that this disease would not go away from me and the people I loved. I had to find an outlet for my anger and my energy. I was determined not to be a victim to this disease and I didn't want to hand on the same legacy to my daughter that was passed on to me. I wanted to help educate other women. That, in fact, has become my cause and my passion for living.

I had read about races that raised funds for other causes. I began discussions with the executive director of the Y-Me National Breast Cancer Organization. With the help and support of many people, the Y-Me Race against Breast Cancer has become our largest fundraiser. The 2002 Race, with more than 30,000 runners and walkers, raised $1.8 million to educate and support women and families.

I believe with Martin Luther King that if we have the courage to create our dreams, they will happen. It happens for me each Mother's Day when thousands of survivors, families and friends arrive in Chicago's Grant Park. It is magnificent—and I am not surprised. At the Race we feel support and positive energy. We know that alone we are runners, but together we are a movement.

—Margaret Harte

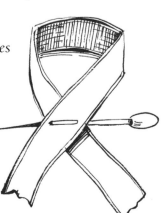

Saint Anthony of Padua
patron of lost items

ANTHONY OF PADUA, A DOCTOR OF THE CHURCH, IS ALSO called "the approachable saint" or the "saint of little things." For centuries people have sought his assistance when they lose or misplace things. In the midst of their worry or panic, they pray the words inscribed in the border of this drawing.

Saint Anthony is associated with Padua, Italy, but he was actually from Portugal. He came to Italy when his ship was forced off course by a storm and landed there. The charismatic Franciscan friar Anthony was the most renowned preacher of his day. One day, there was no one around to hear his sermon, so he preached to the fish in the nearby lake. They came to the surface and poked their heads above the water so they could hear his eloquent words. That is why his halo in this drawing is the aquarium behind his head.

In art, Saint Anthony is traditionally depicted holding the baby Jesus, who in this picture holds the keys and glasses Anthony is searching for! On the back of the envelope on the table are the letters "S.A.G." for "Saint Anthony Guide." People sometimes inscribe these initials on their letters to prevent their getting lost in the mail.

Why is Anthony associated with lost articles? One story suggests a reason: When a young novice stole Anthony's book of psalms, Anthony prayed for its safe return, and the thief had a change of heart. Another reason is that when people heard him preach, they sought to amend their lives. The two sheep in the drawing remind us that when we are feeling lost ourselves, Jesus the Good Shepherd will always manage to find us.

Saint Anthony's feast is June 13.

In the parish where I worked, we invoked Saint Anthony sparingly, trying not to wear out his favors. But every so often, something was lost, things were looking dire, and someone would voice the prayer: "Saint Anthony, Saint Anthony, please come around, for something is lost that needs to be found"—or, in more desperate situations, "Tony, Tony, help me please, Tony, Tony, find my keys."

We all had stories of amazing findings, not just of keys but of large checks and almost-invisible contact lenses. But these prayers raised questions for me as well. They could, after all, sound more like superstition than true prayer. And yet I think there may be depths in these prayers to the patron of those who, like me, are so often seeking after what's lost. After all, it's undeniable that after turning to the saint, whether sheepishly or in full confidence, I seem to have an uncanny knack for finding things, often in places where I swear I've already looked. Perhaps Anthony's gift is one of sight, of clearer awareness of what we have and where we are. Or perhaps it's a gift of humility, a surrender of the self-absorbed tension that can close us off to what's outside ourselves waiting to be revealed.

And perhaps Anthony has another lesson for us as well. There have been times when the prayer hasn't worked for me. Then I find myself not rejoicing like the woman in Luke who finds her lost coin, but struggling to let go. Perhaps this is Anthony's greatest work: to receive the prayers of seekers whose search can't be satisfied and help them surrender. This is the great work, in fact, of our spiritual lives, the work of all of us who lose not only checks, keys and contact lenses, but things far more precious: love and youth, health and hopes, the beauty of every season and every earthly thing. Perhaps Saint Anthony can be our patron when we have to let go of whatever we have held dear and find in its absence a deeper love, a truer faith.

—Anita Houck

3

Saint Bernadette
patron of people with asthma

SAINT BERNADETTE SOUBIROUS GREW UP IN DIRE POVERTY. Her family lived in the filthy basement of a dilapidated building in Lourdes, France. She was undernourished and suffered all her life with poor health. In school, she had difficulty keeping up with her studies and was labeled lazy by her teachers, a label that stuck with her even as an adult.

From the time she was six years old she had asthma, which she later called her "instrument of penance." Frequent, sometimes violent, flare-ups of asthma set her back in school and limited her activities. Because of her delicate health, Bernadette almost did not go out with her sister and a friend to gather firewood one cold February day. It was at the desolate grotto used as the town dump that Bernadette saw and spoke with "a lady wearing a lovely white dress with a bright belt. On top of each of her feet was a pale yellow rose, the same color as her rosary beads." Over the course of eighteen visions, the lady revealed herself to Bernadette as the Immaculate Conception.

At one point the lady instructed Bernadette to drink from the stream. Not seeing a stream, she began to dig in the ground and a spring of water appeared. Almost immediately, this water was known to have healing powers. Since then, people from all over the world have come to bathe in the healing waters of Lourdes, and the grotto has become one of the most popular pilgrimage sites.

As a result of the visions and the discovery of the spring, Bernadette unwillingly became a celebrity. Over the next several years, steady streams of visitors disturbed her privacy. Even after she entered a convent at the age of 22, she was not left alone. Often, as she answered these many visitors' endless questions, her asthma would flare up. Bernadette died of tuberculosis at the age of 36. Her simple faith prompted the words painted in the border of this drawing.

Saint Bernadette's feast is April 16.

I found out that I had asthma when I was six years old and in the first grade. In the beginning, when I didn't know what was wrong with me, I would wake up in the middle of the night coughing and not able to breathe. I would feel petrified and call for my mother.

One day in school, while I was sitting at my desk, my face and lips turned blue and I couldn't catch my breath. I was terrified. My mom took me to the doctor, who told me I had asthma. I didn't really understand what that meant in the first grade. I got to second grade and had difficulty breathing when I ran fast in track, and I got a little more scared about this asthma disease. Not being able to breathe seemed to be happening a lot.

I was getting ready for the third grade when I had a very serious asthma attack that put me in the hospital for a week. I was really afraid about my condition. I had breathing tubes attached to my nose and an intravenous line attached to my arm. It was hard for the doctors to get my oxygen levels up so that I wouldn't need the breathing tubes any more. I prayed that God would help my asthma get better so I could go home and start third grade.

I have had asthma for five years now and I have learned a lot. Having this illness has taught me how to overcome obstacles and realize that God will help me get through rough times. Now my asthma is under control because I take several medicines every day. Asthma hasn't kept me back either: I play basketball and soccer all year long. Praying to God has helped me deal with my asthma because I know God has heard my prayers and has taught me to accept it. I also think that having Bernadette as my middle name has helped a lot too.

—*Jacqueline Bernadette Coppola*

Saint Blase
patron of people with throat ailments

BLASE WAS RAISED IN A WEALTHY ARMENIAN FAMILY, NAMED a bishop at an early age and later became a martyr of the early church. Among the few things known about him is that he took refuge in a cave during a period of Christian persecution. There he befriended sick animals and gained renown as an animal healer. Once he persuaded a wolf not to eat a poor woman's pig. The woman later visited Blase in prison and brought him food and two candles.

Blase was imprisoned and sentenced to death by the Roman emperor Licinius. On the way to his execution, he stopped to save the life of a young boy who was choking on a fish bone. Ever since, Blase has been prayed to in times of throat trouble.

Here Bishop Blase, dressed in red vestments to symbolize martyrdom, blesses the throat of a young girl. The words of this common blessing, given in church every year on his feast day, are in the border. Two crossed candles are used for this blessing and remind us of the poor woman who brought Blase the gift of light in the darkness.

Saint Blase's feast is February 3.

If you want to learn to sing well, join a church choir. I did in sixth grade. I remember the chill in the church those winter mornings, Sister Christopher at the organ and getting my throat blessed on the feast of Saint Blase. I am careful to protect my throat because to me singing is as necessary as breathing. I don't smoke. I wear scarves and loose necklaces and unencumbered necklines. A clear throat is as necessary to a singer as water is to a swimmer.

At home, music was our saving grace. If Broadway musicals and Peter, Paul and Mary weren't on the turntable, classical music was on the radio, especially the Saturday afternoon opera broadcasts that my mother listened to as she peeled potatoes. I learned to sing harmony to distinguish my voice from my sisters'.

In sixth grade, I won a talent show. In eighth grade, I told my friends I was going to be an opera singer and a writer. In high school, I sang the lead roles in musicals, and in college, I studied voice and got a degree in performance.

I found I wasn't interested solely in the classical tradition, which I believed sought perfection over expression. Folk music's exotic melodies and earthy rhythms had greater appeal to me. So I sang Irish folk songs for a time. Now I sing for my livelihood. I choose my own songs and write some too.

The birth of my daughter Epiphania sixteen years ago was a turning point for me. When her birth was imminent my doctor told me: Sing her out. Nia was born easily as I emitted ecstatic sounds of joy (and relief).

A beautiful voice is a miracle. That my throat, lungs and mouth can create something so sublime is a wonder to me, and I am grateful.

—Jamie O'Reilly

Saint Camillus de Lellis
patron of people with AIDS

A SOLDIER OF FORTUNE, A CONSTANT GAMBLER, SIX FEET SIX inches tall, with a terrible temper. This was Camillus de Lellis when he went off to fight against the Turks.

Camillus was wounded in battle; when the wound refused to heal he went into the hospital. In those days, hospitals were not the clean places we know today, with professional nurses and skilled workers. During Camillus' stay in the hospital, he began to work as a nurse. And he experienced a change of heart. He sought to bring compassion and love to the sick and injured. When the pain in his leg made walking impossible, Camillus crawled from bed to bed to visit the patients in whose faces he always saw the face of Christ.

With the encouragement of his spiritual director, Saint Philip Neri, Camillus founded the order of the Servants of the Sick, who changed the world of nursing care. Because of his experience in battle, Camillus was inspired to organize the first field hospital and ambulances for soldiers. He and his brother ministers to the sick roamed the streets and caves of Rome to find plague victims and carry them back to safe, clean hospitals.

Here Camillus plays cards with some patients in an AIDS clinic. He holds in his hands the king of hearts. Around his neck is a red cross, the symbol sewn on the front of the habits worn by his order of brothers. The angel mobile recalls that Camillus is often depicted with an angel as a companion on his nursing rounds.

Saint Camillus de Lellis's feast is July 14.

In the summer of 1983 I worked as a psychotherapist in Ann Arbor, Michigan. I was asked to visit a man who had been diagnosed with AIDS. His name was Jeff and he was gravely ill. At the nurses' station on his floor I was stopped and told to gown up and to put on gloves and a mask. As I came into his room, Jeff slowly looked toward the door and then closed his eyes again. After I introduced myself and told him the reason for my visit, I sat quietly with him for a while. He kept his eyes closed. After a while I asked Jeff if everyone entering his room wore the same get-up, and he said yes. I took off my mask and said, "Jeff, look at my face." He opened his eyes and stared at me. Then he smiled. This first experience with a person with AIDS seems to be the one I still hold on to with the most clarity.

In 1988 I became ill with early symptoms of HIV, and four years later it developed into full-blown AIDS. Long ago the Holy Spirit had granted me the grace to know that God loves me completely as a gay man. This faith has guided me in my work with many other people with HIV infection, as well as during several episodes when I've approached my own death. I continue to live this grace and to feel my vocation in service to others— trying to look at them as God looks at me, face to unmasked face.

—William Hocker

Saint Dymphna
patron of people with mental illness

FOR CENTURIES, DYMPHNA HAS BEEN A FRIEND OF THOSE who suffer mental and emotional distress. Dymphna lived in the seventh century but didn't become popular until seven hundred years later, when her relics were discovered in Belgium.

What we know of Dymphna is based on legend. According to the story, she was born in Ireland and strongly resembled her beautiful mother, who died when Dymphna was young. Her father, insane with grief, wanted to marry her. On the advice of her priest, Dymphna fled to Belgium with some companions but her father followed her. When she refused his advances, he murdered her.

When Dymphna's relics were discovered centuries later, they brought miraculous healing to people with epilepsy and with mental illness. An asylum was built on the site where her relics were found and the town became a pilgrimage site. Dymphna, whose life was so affected by her father's mental illness, was reborn as a patron saint!

Here, standing before a poster of Vincent van Gogh's painting "Starry Night," Dymphna is engaged in art therapy. The artist van Gogh suffered emotional disturbance, but he saw the night stars and sunflowers as signs of God's protective presence. Their light and brightness bring us hope, lift our spirits, and remind us that anything is possible with God— even healing our darkest inner night with the light of the stars.

Saint Dymphna's feast is May 15.

When I was small, I would sometimes drive with my father to a place in the country. We would pick up a friend of my grandmother and she would spend the day with us. I remember that Zia Christina sat very still and quiet in our living room while my mother and Nana Angelina prepared dinner. Zia Christina would stare and smile, mumbling in Italian to no one in particular. After dinner, the adults would include Zia in their conversations and she would appear to hear, but rarely speak. Once after taking her home I asked Nana why Christina behaved the way she did. She said that Zia and people like her were praying because they had seen the face of God.

Long after Nana died, I worked at that same "place in the country," which was a state facility for the chronically mentally ill. I remembered her words and wondered at the cost of seeing God. I worked with people like Christina, people whose mental illnesses were so severe that they could not benefit from medication. Many made poor transitions from the hospital to the community and eventually were abandoned, as many of the mentally ill still are today.

We see them on the streets, and we may try to speak to them or they to us. They may hear not our voices but other voices. Do they fear us when we try to speak to them? Do we fear them? We may wonder if they will survive the day. We may work with them, assist them in the hope that they may be able to care for themselves. Are they aware of their plight, or is their focus on another time and place? Have they seen the face of God, or should we see God's face in theirs?

—Thomas J. Como

Saint Elizabeth Ann Seton
patron of widows and single parents

ELIZABETH ANN SETON, THE FIRST SAINT BORN IN THE United States, founder of a religious order, and a great teacher who started the Catholic education system in the United States, was a convert to Catholicism.

At nineteen, Elizabeth married William Seton, a wealthy New York businessman. Their elegant home, where they entertained George Washington and Alexander Hamilton, still stands on Wall Street today, dwarfed between two modern skyscrapers.

After nine years of marriage, William's business and health were failing. Together they traveled to Italy in hopes that the warm climate would ease his tuberculosis, but to no avail. He died there in 1803. Elizabeth was a widow with five children and no means of support. While in Italy, Elizabeth was impressed by their Catholic friends' devotion and faith. She soon converted to Catholicism, much to the distress of her family and friends in the United States.

Back in New York, she founded a small school to earn some money for herself and her children. In time, she was led in faith to found the Sisters of Charity in Emmitsburg, Maryland, and she became a champion of Catholic education for all children, regardless of race, gender or class.

In this drawing Elizabeth huddles with her five children while a storm rages outside. She gathers them in a red, white and blue quilt, a symbol of her American heritage. The quotation in the border reminds us that Elizabeth Ann Seton believed that we should grow, not be destroyed, through suffering.

Saint Elizabeth Ann Seton's feast is January 4.

On July 27, 1995, Jim, my husband of 23 years, died of the injuries he sustained in a motor vehicle accident. At the time our five children were between 11 and 20 years old. It was so difficult to comprehend that this vibrant man could be gone only a few short hours after the accident.

Two major thoughts continuously ran through my mind after Jim's death: We will survive this. We need to be the people we were meant to be.

This was the first time in my life that my faith had been truly tested. I was overwhelmed by the magnitude of what Jim's death meant. I was worried that I would not be able to adequately care for my children and respond to their needs. In time I began to sense that God was grieving with me and giving me what I needed. I felt God's presence in the support we received from family, friends and even strangers. As the days and weeks and months passed I was able to support and comfort my children in their anger, grief and pain.

I will always feel the pain of Jim's death and his physical absence in our daily lives. Yet I am able to celebrate his life and be grateful for all he has given us. I am especially thankful for the strength God gave me and the people God sent to love, comfort and hold us. My greatest joy is to see that my children have grown into the young adults they were meant to be. They are kind and caring young men and women, not angry or bitter. We are a close family who are able to show our care and love for each other.

In the book of Sirach we read, "These were godly men, whose righteous deeds have not been forgotten. . . . Their bodies are buried in peace, but their name lives on generation after generation. The assembly declares their wisdom and the congregation proclaims their praise."

Since Jim's death, we live this.

—*Patricia Bolin*

Saint Felicity
patron of people with infertility

Saint Catherine of Sweden
patron of people experiencing miscarriage

FELICITY IS USUALLY DEPICTED WITH PERPETUA BECAUSE they died side by side as martyrs. Perpetua, a young noble-woman in North Africa, was a Christian convert along with several friends and her servant Felicity. Perpetua wrote a beautifully detailed account of their religious journey and time in prison, which is now considered one of the treasures of the early church.

Felicity was eight months pregnant when the women were imprisoned, and Roman law stipulated that she could not be killed in the arena until after the baby was born. Knowing that she would be killed eventually, and wanting to die with her friends, she prayed through the night before their scheduled execution that her baby would be prematurely born. The next morning, after a difficult labor, her baby was delivered and handed over to family members. Soon after, Felicity and Perpetua were sent to the arena. After exchanging a kiss of peace, they were killed.

Catherine is the fourth of Saint Bridget of Sweden's eight children. She traveled to Rome with her mother where they befriended another saint, Catherine of Siena. After her mother's death, Catherine returned to Sweden to head the monastery her mother had founded. It is no longer known why she is patron of women who have suffered miscarriage, but it is the tradition.

In this drawing, the two saints listen for new life inside Felicity's womb. Between them is a statue of a black Madonna, recalling Felicity's African heritage. The bull mask behind Felicity's head recalls the means of her martyrdom. Around her neck she wears a pendant that resembles the letter "M" for Mary, which is also a fertility symbol from North Africa, her homeland.

Saint Felicity's feast is March 7.
Saint Catherine of Sweden's feast is March 24.

Most of us naturally assume that we will be able to have children easily when we feel we are ready. What a shock it is to learn that we may never bear the children we desire. I am an infertile woman. My husband and I tried to have a child for seven years, but our efforts failed. I am also a social worker. In my professional practice, I often work with infertile couples. Their struggles and ours have been strikingly similar; this is an age-old ordeal, recorded even in the Bible.

Most of all, infertility is an experience of loss— of the child we keep hoping to conceive, of feelings of normalcy, of a sense of control over our lives, of emotional well-being, and much more. When we seek medical assistance, we also lose privacy in our most intimate experiences as a couple. Trying to help us fulfill our dreams, doctors guide every step of the reproductive process. They give us drugs with powerful side effects and often treat us with invasive medical and surgical procedures. But despite the wonders of modern medicine, treatment frequently fails. The disappointment is crushing, and even strong faith can be shaken.

Infertility puts great stress on a marriage. Some relationships flounder, but couples who learn to meet its challenges become stronger. Understanding support from family, friends and clergy can be of much help. Ultimately couples need to heal from this difficult life experience, whether or not they go on to become parents through successful treatment or adoption.

—Ann M. Bergart, PhD, LCSW

Saint Genevieve
patron in times of national disaster

IN THE EARLY MIDDLE AGES THE FRANKS BESEIGED PARIS. Genevieve slipped through their blockade and led an expedition to the nearby town of Troyes. There they loaded boats with corn, barley and wheat, and smuggled it back into the city for the starving Parisians.

This courageous act was no surprise to anyone who knew her. When she was only seven years old, a bishop gave Genevieve a medal of the cross and prophesied that she would be a great leader. Genevieve was widely known for her gift of prophecy and foretold disasters and invasions. Once she led a large group of women in fasting and prayer to divert the invading armies of Attila the Hun. As a result, Saint Genevieve is not only the patron of Paris, but the saint to pray to in times of national disaster.

Inspired by the scenes of rescue workers rushing to duty in the aftermath of September 11, 2001, this drawing shows Genevieve at the prow of a rescue boat bringing cereal and grain to a city after a contemporary disaster. Her halo is a life preserver on the dock behind her. In the border, Psalm 78:24 refers to manna, the food sent from heaven when the Israelites were wandering in the desert. Manna is the bread of angels and heroes and all rescue workers.

Saint Genevieve's feast is January 3.

Any day could bring word to Catholic Relief Services of a new disaster: a flood in India leaves thousands homeless, an earthquake in El Salvador buries a village in a mudslide, a lava flow in the Congo destroys hundreds of homes, war in Sudan sends hundreds seeking refuge. In such disasters CRS immediately responds by providing food, clothing and shelter, and just as important, physical and psychological support to people caught in the worst situations. At the heart of this work of CRS is a commitment to the gospel of Jesus Christ that is lived out in service to the poor in the world. I work for this amazing international organization of the Roman Catholic church in the United States because of my own commitment to the gospel.

In my travels for CRS I have met the people we serve and the dedicated staff. I have heard mothers weep over the death of their children, heard children cry out for justice, and witnessed the devastation of floods. The challenge is to bring the stories of these people to Catholics in the United States in the hope of building solidarity among the people of the world.

I recently sat with a grandmother in the hills of Uganda who had lost seven of her ten children to AIDS. Her husband was dead and she was taking care of her six orphaned grandchildren. In spite of such tragedy, she lived in thankfulness and hope. One of the great lessons I am learning through the people I meet is to give thanks for life itself.

As I listen to the stories of people living through incredible disasters, I have been moved by the depth of faith in their lives. I have witnessed the power of love in communities that support one another during times of trouble. I have come to know the goodness of people, especially in such times. But most important, I am struck by the hope that continues to live in people, even in the midst of disaster. Surely this is grace!

—*Kathy Brown*

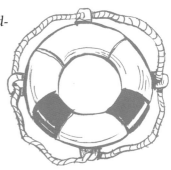

Saint Giles
patron of people with disabilities

SAINT GILES, A 7TH-CENTURY FRENCH HERMIT, LIVED IN A cave in a forest. He is often portrayed with a deer because it is said that God sent him a doe to provide him with milk. One day, King Flavius was hunting in the forest and shot an arrow at the deer but hit Giles's leg instead. The king, who sent doctors to care for Giles's wound, began to visit Giles for spiritual advice. Giles's reputation as a wise and healing guide spread, and the king built a monastery there.

Traditional symbols for Saint Giles are the deer, which we see here in the patch on his sleeve, and the arrows, which are in his backpack. In this rendering of Saint Giles, his wheelchair does not confine his spirit! Like the tails of the kite soaring above, Giles reminds us of true freedom. Even if physical conditions keep us from full mobility, when our spirits are free, we can do anything. God will raise us up on the wings of an eagle—or maybe a seagull!

Saint Giles's feast is September 1.

When I was a boy it was my job, along with my older sister, Anne, to carry Oliver to the bathtub. Oliver could not walk.

I remember the bright light in Oliver's room as our mother opened the windows each morning. Oliver could not see.

Sometimes, when school was difficult, or I was sad, I would sit next to Oliver and tell him of my woes. Oliver could not hear.

When Oliver was born, the doctors told our mother and father that Oliver would never be able to learn anything for he had no intellect. Most of the world said that Oliver was useless, retarded, a burden. Our mother and father decided to call Oliver wonderful, rich, a gift.

On bath day, Anne would hold Oliver's legs and I would hold his arms, and she and I would gently lift him from his bed and carry him down the hall.

I remember Anne and me slowly lowering Oliver into the bathtub and watching our father gently wash his crooked body.

I knew that Oliver was a physical mess, but even as a boy, I knew that his inside self, his soul-self, was an Olympic star because our parents were able to see Oliver's strength and power.

When I look back to those years of long ago, I clearly understand Oliver's power to heal in his silence as I spoke at his bedside about my troubles. Today I clearly understand Oliver's strength to bind my sister and me forever as we carried him to the bathtub.

It may sound impossible, but the weakest people in our lives have the greatest power, for it is they who teach us the power of silence, compassion, generosity simply by being among us as they reach out and say "Will you feed me? Will you bathe me? Will you love me?"

—Christopher de Vinck

Saint Gregory the Wonderworker
patron against floods and earthquakes

SAINT GREGORY THE WONDERWORKER WAS BORN ABOUT THE year 213 to noble parents. His plans to study law changed after he met Origen, one of the fathers of the church, with whom he studied philosophy and scripture.

It is said that when Gregory became bishop of Caesarea there were only 17 Christians there, and when he died there were only 17 people who weren't Christians there. Not only did he make many converts to Christianity, he also healed the sick and foretold the future. He is believed to be the first person to have received a vision of the Virgin Mary.

Gregory's reputation as a worker of miracles is based on many marvels in his life. Once, two brothers were quarreling over how to divide a piece of land that had a lake on it. Gregory prayed, and the lake dried up. He stopped a local river's frequent floods by planting his bishop's staff near its edge. The staff took root, and the river never rose past that tree.

After his death, his body ended up in southern Italy, where the people built a shrine. In times of earthquake and flood, they would pray to him for protection, and after a while he became the official patron of those particular calamities.

In this drawing Gregory is standing in a doorframe, the safest spot during an earthquake. A painting of Noah's ark hangs where the wall once stood as a reminder of the first great flood that covered the earth. Saint Gregory's umbrella hasn't survived, nor the walls of his house, but like Noah and the animals, Gregory and his friends are alive and well. They gather beneath a rainbow, an eternal sign of peace.

Gregory the Wonderworker's feast is November 17.

On October 17, 1989, at 5:03 in the afternoon, the ground in northern California shook violently. It was the magnitude 7.1 Loma Prieta earthquake.

I was at work when the earth quaked. I will never forget the sheer force and power of those first few seconds. My building rocked like a seesaw and ceiling tiles crumbled to the floor. I panicked and along with my co-workers ran to the outside of the office building.

The normal 20-minute commute to my home took five hours. When I arrived home in the Santa Cruz mountains, I found my house was in shambles. Broken glass, demolished streets and frightened neighbors were everywhere. This is when I began to pray. I lost my possessions, my dear cat was lost for over a week, but I was lucky—my life was spared. Somehow, amid the rubble, I continued on.

During this time of uncertainty my family rushed to my side. My community and friends were a source of comfort, care and relief during this terrible and violent act of nature.

The powerful force that rocked the earth's foundation gave me ultimate strength. With the prayers and the knowledge of Saint Gregory, I feel that I too can move boulders. It is in faith that I believe in Jesus and in my guardian angel who have brought me safely through.

—Melissa Collingwood

Saint James

patron of people with arthritis

JAMES AND HIS BROTHER JOHN WERE MENDING THEIR fishing nets on the beach when Jesus called them to be his apostles. They dropped what they were doing and followed him. These two brothers, whom Jesus nicknamed "sons of thunder," were part of his inner circle and along with Peter were chosen to witness Jesus' transfiguration.

James, the first apostle to be martyred, was beheaded by King Herod Agrippa. Legend has it that because James had traveled to Spain to preach the gospel, after his death his remains were carried there by boat. A horse on the shore was frightened by the sight of the miraculous boat and plunged into the sea, taking its rider with it. But instead of drowning, the horse and rider galloped back to the beach, covered with seashells. The basilica built at the site, Santiago de Compostela, is a famous pilgrimage site. Over time, many people who suffered with arthritis began to report that they were healed at roadside shrines to Saint James along the famous pilgrim route.

Artists began to depict Saint James with scallop shells pinned to his tunic and wide-brimmed traveling hat. Because pilgrims walk to Santiago from all over the world, James was given a walking stick and a gourd of water. Today's pilgrims to this shrine in northern Spain, shown here at the top of the cliff, continue the tradition and carry a walking stick with a water gourd and wear shells on their shirts and wide-brimmed hats.

Saint James' feast is July 25.

I was diagnosed with rheumatoid arthritis 34 years ago, at the age of 27. At first I didn't really know what to think. All I knew was that I felt sick and in a lot of pain, and my parents and siblings were very concerned. The early years were especially difficult. My disease was unrelenting as it attacked one joint after another in my body. I worried about ending up in a wheelchair or being completely crippled. As time went on, my condition stabilized and now is controlled by medication. However, I realized that life was going to be different than I had envisioned, and I had to come to grips with the fact that I had a chronic disease.

In spite of the hardships arthritis has brought me, it has also been a gift. I have learned to put my trust in God and I know that he will give me strength. I no longer worry about the future. I know that God will be with me. When I am having a particularly bad time, I try to be optimistic and pray that it will pass and that I will feel better soon.

Having arthritis has necessitated my asking for help and relying on others at times. This is not easy to do but I have been blessed with a wonderful support system. I've had great doctors to care for me. Most importantly, my family and friends have always been there for me. I am fortunate because my situation has allowed me to know how much I am loved. This has enriched my life, and I know my personal relationships are stronger and more rewarding than many people's.

I have tried not to let illness dominate my life. It has definitely strengthened my character. I have a positive attitude and I try to maintain a sense of humor through all that rheumatoid arthritis entails. In the broad picture, I have a very full life and so much for which to be thankful.

—Elizabeth Fox

Saint Jane de Chantal
patron of people who grieve

NOT MANY PEOPLE SUFFER AS MANY LOSSES IN THEIR LIVES as Jane de Chantal. Her mother died when Jane was a little girl, and she was raised by her adoring father, a lawyer and prominent politician. After eight happy years of marriage, Jane's noble husband was killed by a friend in a hunting accident. As her husband was dying, he begged Jane to forgive the man who had accidentally shot him. It was many years before she could bring herself to do so, but eventually she did—and even became the godmother of his child.

Jane was a widow at 28, with four children under five including a week-old baby. When she recovered from her grief, she took up the study of herbal medicine and midwifery. She brought the sick into her home and nursed them back to health. She baked bread for the poor in an oven she had built so that bread could be made in quantity around the clock.

Of all the losses in her life, she sometimes said that the most difficult was the death of her best friend, Francis de Sales, with whom she founded the Order of the Visitation in 1610. She outlived him by twenty years.

Here we see Saint Jane in a reflective moment surrounded by pictures of her loved ones who have died. The single pink tulip directs us to the empty chair at her table and the rising sun outside. Flowers on her scarf and wallpaper remind us that new life always follows death. Jane de Chantal's life is an example of healing and forgiveness. She shows us how to accept grief and learn from it, perhaps even how to turn our losses into gain for others.

Saint Jane de Chantal's feast is August 18.

The day our family gathered for my granddaughter Sophia's baptism, my youngest son Peter, then 27, stood beneath the church's beautiful Tiffany window portraying Jesus with the children. I quickly took his picture so I could forever cherish this image.

The next morning my beautiful Peter was dead, a suicide. He left a long tape and several notes trying to help us understand why he could no longer endure. He said it was time "to go home."

Plunged into unbearable pain, I couldn't even pray. When I developed the photo I had taken I was strangely comforted. I felt Peter was somehow raised, there with Jesus, one of his children. My grieving was soul-deep, but that image brought me peace.

Then two years later, my grief knew no bounds—my son John and his wife Nancy had been murdered. I begged God for help, and found it again in that image, somehow "seeing" that Peter, John and Nancy were all there with Jesus and the children.

I knew then I could be strong, for I had felt Jesus' hand on my heart, pouring his grace into my body and soul and redesigning my faith. I would no longer question "Why?" and "Why me?" My new faith meant letting go of those questions and asking a better one, "Lord, who will you help me become now that I'll never be who I was?"

I know I will grieve forever for my loved ones because I miss them so. But my grieving rests in a chariot of joy, because I see Jesus with the children— with my children—in that wondrous place he has prepared for all of us in his endless embrace of love.

—Antoinette Bosco

Saint Josephine Bakhita
patron against racial discrimination

JOSEPHINE WAS A HAPPY NINE-YEAR-OLD PLAYING WITH HER friends outside their village in Sudan in 1869 when she was kidnapped by slave traders. She never saw her parents or family again, though she lived another seventy years. She endured the horrors of slavery, being sold and resold, tortured, and worked to exhaustion. Once her master beat her unconscious, and she lay near death for a month. Another time, the wife of her Turkish owner had over sixty tattoos cut into her skin with a razor blade, then rubbed them with salt so they would make permanent scars.

When she was fourteen, Josephine was sold to a kindly Italian diplomat. He brought her to Venice and treated her well. When he and his wife traveled on business, their daughter and Josephine stayed at a convent in Venice. There Josephine was impressed by the kindness of the Sisters of Charity, learned of God and was baptized. When the diplomat was re-assigned to Africa and asked her to accompany the family there, she decided to stay in Italy and become a sister herself.

Josephine became widely known outside the walls of her convent world. She told people that she forgave her captors and harbored no hatred for them because the misery they inflicted on her led her to Jesus. The Italians affectionately referred to her as Mother Moretta, "our black mother." People sought her wisdom and gentle, kind nature, especially during the harsh years of two world wars. At her death, thousands of people lined up to pay their respects.

Walking in front of Saint Josephine we see Ruby Bridges, the first African American child to attend a formerly all-white school when segregation was outlawed in 1960. The border of African textiles bears a quote from Josephine. Her life and spirit are inspiring examples of reconciliation with our enemies and of faith in a God who has children of many colors.

Saint Josephine Bakhita's feast is February 8.

At a young age I became keenly aware of something that made me different from the rest of my family. People have always asked questions about my appearance, but I rarely give a straight answer. I don't like to make public that I am both adopted and biracial in casual conversation. The most hurtful thing that people say about my family is, "Oh, so they're not your real *family." I respond, "Of course they're my* real *family. They're the only family I've ever known."*

Growing up in an Irish Catholic neighborhood in Chicago, I was the only black student in a school of 400. After I was called a nigger in the sixth grade, my parents decided it was time for us to move to a more integrated community. I cannot thank them enough for that decision. I had a wonderful experience in the Oak Park, Illinois, schools and was awarded an academic scholarship for black students to Xavier University in Cincinnati.

There is still racial discrimination, both subtle and very open, in America. I've noticed store clerks following my every move while ignoring my white friends shopping with me. Only two years ago, I witnessed a Ku Klux Klan rally in the busiest intersection of downtown Cincinnati. This frightening sight made me wonder why free speech and assembly are granted in this country to groups that openly advocate hatred and both racial and religious discrimination.

I am well aware that the discrimination I have experienced in my life is very minor compared to what so many other Americans have faced. Slavery was abolished some 140 years ago, but we still have evidence of deep-rooted hatred and racial discrimination in all areas of the United States.

—Sarah Doherty

BLESSED ARE THOSE WHO HUNGER AND THIRST FOR RIGHTEOUSNESS FOR THEY WILL BE FILLED MT 5:6

Saint Juan Diego
patron of the disenfranchised

THE STORY OF JUAN DIEGO, A POOR AZTEC INDIAN WHO worked as a field hand and matmaker, reminds us of God's love for the poor and outcast of society.

One morning in 1531, as Juan Diego walked the many miles to Mass, he had a vision of Mary. She spoke to him in his own language, Nahuatl, calling him "my little one," and told him that she, the mother of all the poor, hears the cries of the weak and despised in this world. She asked him to go to the bishop to say that she wanted a shrine built on that site. He answered that he was "a nobody," but did as she requested.

After several more appearances, she gave him fresh roses in the middle of winter and imprinted an image of herself on his *tilma,* or cape. When the bishop saw these, he knelt down and asked to be shown the place where the visions occurred.

The place where Juan Diego had his visions was lifeless and barren, much like the trash-strewn vacant lot shown here. Today the shrine of Our Lady of Guadalupe in Mexico City is the second most popular pilgrim site in the world. Visitors from around the globe come to see the tilma of Juan Diego and to have their hope restored in the God who raises the poor and lowly above the the rich and powerful.

Saint Juan Diego's feast is December 9.

My great-grandparents arrived in Wisconsin from Germany in 1866. When August became ill soon after that, Louise summoned a doctor, who prescribed medicine to be given in drops. But because they didn't understand English, Louise gave August his medicine in teaspoons, and the overdose killed him. For generations since, my family has been involved in teaching. The inability to read or write disenfranchises people and I work to help adults overcome this.

The Tolton Center for Adult Education is named after Augustus Tolton, the first known black priest in the United States. The Tolton Center serves people 16 years or older and their families. Many are among the 21% of Americans who function at the lowest level of literacy. This means adults who cannot read the instructions on a medicine bottle, a story to a child, a note from the teacher, mail, newspapers, a voting ballot and much more.

Some of our success stories include a 64-year-old woman who wanted to read the Bible; a 40-year-old man who learned to read to pass the driver's test so that he could drive a Pepsi distributor's trucks; a 17-year-old dropout who earned a GED and entered college; a young mother who learned to read to her children; a 50-year-old woman who found her voice and joined a writer's group.

Not everyone achieves his or her goals. Some disappear just as they are making progress. But change happens incrementally—perhaps next time.

I am inspired by Paulo Freire, who worked with the poor in Brazil and pointed out that education either works to preserve the status quo, or it is about the work of human liberation.

—*Susan Carew Perez*

Saint Jude Thaddeus
patron of desperate situations

JUDE THADDEUS, ONE OF THE TWELVE APOSTLES, IS AMONG the most popular of all the saints. Countless people in difficult and hopeless situations have turned to Saint Jude for help.

The brother of James the Less and Simon, he might have been also a nephew of Mary, which would make him Jesus' cousin. The Letter of Jude, the shortest book in the New Testament, is attributed to him. It is said that Simon and Jude traveled to Persia, or modern-day Iran, to preach the gospel, and that is where they were martyred.

The reason Jude became associated with hopeless or desperate causes is simple. His name is similar to that of Judas Iscariot who betrayed Jesus. Some say that this prevented people from praying to him. To get over this confusion, Jude works extra hard to answer prayers. Part of the popular tradition is for petitioners to plead for Jude's help in a public way, so it is not uncommon to see prayers to him printed in the classified ads of the newspaper.

What could be more hopeless than watering a stick and expecting it to grow? Doing it in winter with a leaky hose that's not connected to the faucet. Now that's hopeless! But Saint Jude and his countless devotees remind us time and again that nothing is impossible with God.

Saint Jude Thaddeus' feast is October 28.

The needs are great and the cries are desperate: Pray for a family of five in which one son has died from a rare disease, the father and another son have tested positive for the same disease, another is being tested for it, and the mother suffers from migraine headaches. Pray for support as we await an organ donor and transplant for my sister. Pray for my daughter who is incarcerated, for my son who awaits a judge's verdict. Pray for me and my family for I have been unemployed for some time. Pray that I may recover from addiction. Teens and young adults seek clarity in their interpersonal relationships. We pray for social, political and economic concerns. We share in seemingly impossible grief and lament with others broken by various forms of abuse.

Many people around the world seek the intercession of Saint Jude Thaddeus. People gather for celebrations of the word of God, Mass, and the sacraments of reconciliation and anointing of the sick. Our shrine, the Shrine of Saint Jude in Chicago, provides five annual novenas. These are preached by men and women diverse in racial and cultural experience. Yearly we reply to nearly 100,000 pieces of mail. Electronic visits to our web page and Prayernet increase daily.

Our personal contact and intercession with these Friends of Saint Jude supports them to "persevere in God's love, and welcome the mercy of our Lord Jesus Christ, which leads to eternal life" (Jude 21).

—*Thomas J. Johnston, OP*

Saint Lucy

patron of people with eye disease

SAINT LUCY'S FEAST DAY FALLS IN WINTER WHEN THE DAYS are growing shorter and darker. Because her name means "light," she is associated with festivals of light. In Sweden young girls wear wreaths of candles on their heads to celebrate her feast, much as Lucy wears in the picture here. In Venice, she is the patron saint of the gondoliers who sing "Santa Lucia" as they steer their boats through the canals.

Lucy, who was from Sicily, is one of the virgin martyrs of the early church. She lived during the reign of the emperor Diocletian who tried to have her killed several ways. When he ordered that she be put in a brothel as a child prostitute, her body became unmovable, even by a team of oxen.

There are other reasons why Lucy is associated with eye trouble. When she was martyred, her eyes were torn out, though one legend says that she received her sight again before she died. Whatever the case may be, traditional art shows her holding her eyes on a silver platter.

Here Saint Lucy is portrayed as an ophthalmologist, the doctor who heals our sight. She holds a flashlight in one hand and a test for color blindness in the other. Behind her is today's technology for examining the eyes and a chart that displays a message from the Saint Paul—reminders that we are children of the light and have Christ as our guide through the darkness.

Saint Lucy's feast is December 13.

I am a 25-year survivor of chronic uveitis, iritis and glaucoma. My eye problems began three months after the birth of my daughter. At first, it felt like there was something in my eye, like sand. This feeling lasted about a month, and I visited a local ophthalmologist. I was diagnosed with uveitis, an inflammation in the middle of the eye, which can lead to iritis, an inflammation in the front of the eye. Although uveitis and iritis are treatable with cortisone drops, my inflammation became chronic. The treatment of the inflammation caused cataracts and eventually glaucoma in both eyes. Recently, I had my fifth eye operation. A shunt was placed in my left eye to decrease the pressure of glaucoma. The surgery has reduced the pressure, but my vision has greatly deteriorated, and it is uncertain whether that is permanent.

Living with an illness that limits my ability to perform basic daily tasks has been a trying experience. The power of prayer has lifted and carried me through many bouts of diminished vision. Most recently, after surgery, the inflammation in my right eye flared up and I was unable to drive, read a newspaper or fill out a form. During this time in particular, I learned to lean on others for prayer and support. My friends and family drove me where I needed to go and read for me when I could not. It has been a humbling experience to ask for help, but I believe this has enlightened me to see the face of God in everyone I meet.

—Maryrose Smith

The Magi
patrons of safe travel

SOME OF THE MOST POPULAR CHARACTERS IN THE CHRISTMAS story are the Magi, or wise men. They are mentioned only in the gospel of Matthew, which says that a new star in the east led them to the home of the baby Jesus. Scripture does not record their names and origin, but tradition has assigned them the names of Caspar, Melchior and Balthasar. And as every Christmas crèche shows, they traveled by camel, bringing with them gifts of gold, frankincense and myrrh.

The three wise men, the first Gentiles to worship Jesus, have sometimes been called the first Christian pilgrims. Heeding the warnings of an angel, the Magi didn't return to tell King Herod where the new king was. They took another route home, which ensured their safe travel.

The gifts of the Magi, shown being screened in the metal detector, carry important meaning to the story. Gold, a gift fit for a king, stands for virtue. Frankincense, an incense, has a sweet scent that rises in prayer to God. And myrrh, a perfume used for embalming the dead, foreshadows Christ's death. And, as often happens, even their shoes are carefully checked.

The Magi, strangers from a foreign land who sought the infant Jesus, remind us that all of us can make the journey to God, and that we must help each other along the way.

The feast of the Magi is January 6.

As a flight attendant for a major airline, it is my job to ensure the safely of all the passengers. Safety is the number one concern for flight attendants. Although passengers see us mostly serving meals and beverages and making sure everyone is comfortable during the flight, we are on the alert for any situations that could arise.

Some of the routine concerns for which we are prepared are: What do I do if a passenger becomes ill during the flight? What happens if we go through some turbulence and someone falls and is hurt? How do I comfort someone who is fearful of flying?

Through my training and faith in God I have been able to help people in these times. I administer first aid to ill or injured passengers. By listening, showing concern and praying, I help calm fears. I am always happy to help someone in need and thank God he is with me.

People fly for pleasure, for business and for family obligations. Before every flight I say a prayer to God to keep us safe on our journey. We can also pray to the Magi, patron saints of travel, for their protection and ask them to guide us safely to our destination.

—*Marlena McCarthy*

Saint Margaret Mary Alacoque
patron of people with heart disease

WHEN SAINT MARGARET MARY WAS A LITTLE GIRL, SHE LOVED to pray before the Blessed Sacrament. It was a safe place to "pour out her heart to God in tears," a place of safety far away from her troubled home life. Her father died when she was young and Margaret Mary was forced to live with her harsh uncle and two aunts.

A serious childhood illness left her weak, and all her life she struggled with feelings of low self-esteem. When she was 20 she joined the Order of the Visitation.

In 1673, Saint Margaret Mary had the first of four visions of the Sacred Heart while she was praying alone in the chapel during all-night adoration of the Blessed Sacrament. The superior and the other nuns didn't believe her at first. Her only support came from her Jesuit spiritual director, Saint Claude de la Colombiere, who encouraged her to write detailed accounts of these visions. Through her efforts to let people know of the love of Jesus, devotion to the Sacred Heart spread, first throughout France and then the world.

Margaret Mary is shown in a gym doing aerobic exercises, as all heart patients are supposed to do. The towel around her neck is monogrammed with the initials of her community, VHM, Visitation of Holy Mary. The Sacred Heart of Jesus appears on the video screen while the monitor on her treadmill shows a heart encircled by a crown of thorns, fitting the description of her visions. Another crown of thorns is suggested in the exercise poster behind her head. When we exchange hearts with Jesus, we come to a place of peace and healing that only he can give.

Saint Margaret Mary's feast is October 16.

"*I will take you into the desert and there speak to your heart*" (Hosea 2:16). *Hosea was on hard times when God spoke to him in the desert. God spoke to my heart in the desert too.*

An electrical heart ailment, arrhythmia, put me on hard times. Arrhythmia, an off-beat heart rhythm, is crippling. My desert experience occurred in my own bedroom, where I spent many months waiting to have a special procedure known as an ablation.

At that time I saw everything in terms of the heart. The heart as pump. The heart as feelings. Coeur de Lion, the monarchical magnanimous heart radiating out from itself, large and golden as the sun

The Sacred Heart was among many flashbacks to my childhood during my long sojourn in the desert. The house of my Irish grandmother was a dark old-fashioned place full of hallways and stairways. Impressive to me was a picture gallery room with walls full of family pictures from many generations. There were my uncles in their World War II uniforms, my grandfather on a horse in his dress uniform, gray gloves and baton from the Chicago Fire Department, women in flowing gowns and wedding veils. Everyone she loved was there. In the middle of all these was a large picture of the Sacred Heart, and next to it, President Franklin Roosevelt. There at the center of her world beat the Sacred Heart.

That image of the Sacred Heart became my meditation during this period of heart illness. I saw that divine love is in the deep heart's core. Not just in my core but at the core of everyone and all of us together.

—Lillian Lewis

Saint Maria Goretti
patron of people who have been abused

MARIA GORETTI LIVED WITH HER FAMILY ABOVE AN OLD DAIRY barn on a small Italian farm. A nearby mosquito-infested swamp contributed to her father's early death from malaria, meningitis and typhus. Despite extreme poverty and deprivation (she was too poor to go to school or have toys), Maria was said to have a beautiful, cheerful disposition. While her mother worked on the farm, Maria was responsible for the household duties, including caring for the other children. She cooked the meals and fed them, taught them their prayers and told them stories. All this responsibility made her mature beyond her years, and when she was twelve years old, she looked much older.

One day, while everyone was working in fields far from the house, Maria was outside doing some mending. No one was around to hear her cries for help when Alessandro, the son of the landowner, dragged her into the house and attempted to rape her. As is often the case, she knew her attacker well. When she was young, she had thought of him as her big brother. She resisted him, telling Alessandro that he was offending Jesus, and he stabbed her fourteen times. Maria lingered for twenty hours in the hospital before she died.

When the local priest came to bring her communion, she told him she had forgiven Alessandro, who was soon arrested and sentenced to prison. Eight years later, Maria appeared to Alessandro in a vision. She was standing in a field of flowers wearing a white dress and holding lilies in her hand. He had a conversion of heart and became a Capuchin friar after his release from prison.

When Maria Goretti was declared a saint in 1950, it was the first time that a mother was present at her child's canonization. Sitting next to her was Alessandro. The woman who gave Maria Goretti life and the man who took it away celebrated together the triumph of forgiveness.

Saint Maria Goretti's feast is July 6.

From at least age six to sometime after I was nine, I was kissed, fondled and eventually raped by a man ten years my senior—a man who was such a close and trusted family friend that my parents considered him to be almost another son. I told no one . . . at least not directly. During the years I was being abused, especially after being raped, I desperately wanted my family to notice that something was wrong. I just couldn't face telling them. I was too ashamed, too afraid that I would be labeled a whore since that's what I felt I was. How else could I explain why I hadn't told anyone earlier, why I hadn't stopped him the moment he first touched me inappropriately? Wrongfully believing that I was thus somehow to blame for the abuse, I buried the truth of my experience under layers of hurt, anger, isolation and self-loathing.

Why me? Why anyone? In the face of such a devastating crime—and that's what it is—there are no satisfactory explanations. Nevertheless, to begin to heal it has been necessary for me to try to find some meaning in my experience. The abuse drove me inward in search of answers, and awakened in me both profound compassion and a deep sense of social justice. My greatest desire now is to somehow help others who have been victimized in this way.

It has taken me many years and a tremendous amount of courage to finally face what happened to me. It's frightening, but liberating, too. Finally, I'm telling, and this time I will not be ashamed.

—*Lynne M. Meyer*

Venerable Matt Talbot
patron of people with alcoholism

MATT TALBOT BEGAN DRINKING WHEN HE WAS TWELVE YEARS old. One of twelve children, Matt lived in a slum in Dublin, Ireland. School was out of the question because Matt worked ten hours a day, six days a week, as a delivery boy for a wine merchant. When Matt was older he worked on the docks as his father had done, and as his father had done, after work he would go straight to the pub and spend his wages on drink. What started as a habit escalated into life-threatening disease. More than once Matt even sold his work boots to keep drinking.

When he was 28, he had a change of heart. He went to confession and made a pledge to stop drinking for three months. He went to Mass every morning before work and visited church at the end of the day. He also quit carrying money so he couldn't be tempted to buy liquor. When the three months were up, he renewed his pledge. Matt remained sober the rest of his life. At the same time, he also gave up smoking, and told his friends that was even tougher than alcohol.

Matt stopped hanging around with his old drinking buddies but he eventually returned to all his old haunts to pay back his debts. He was known for his generosity to the poor and his staunch support of laborers. Although he was barely educated, Matt took great pleasure in reading spiritual books. He copied anything that he had difficulty understanding and asked others for help. After 41 years of sobriety, Matt Talbot died of a heart attack on his way to morning Mass.

In this drawing, Venerable Matt gives us the "thumbs up" sign because he has made his pledge and stuck with it. His life encourages us to live one day at a time and not give up on ourselves. But we can't do this alone. Fortified by the humble acknowledgment that we need God's help, we can stand up to anything.

Matt Talbot is remembered on the day he died, June 7.

"We are not saints. The point is that we are willing to grow along spiritual lines. We claim spiritual progress rather than spiritual perfection." Alcoholics Anonymous

I began drinking in my early teens, and I drank almost every day until I was in middle age. I tried to moderate my drinking many times, without success. As is often the case with alcoholics, I lived a life of outward achievement—I was a successful lawyer with a large, loving family—as I sank into the depths of alcoholism. Eventually, my vision was so narrowed that my only goal was to hoard enough money to support my family after I was gone. I was powerless in the face of alcohol, alone in despair, watching my life slip away.

In 1989, defeated, I turned to AA. Slowly, haltingly, I learned to trust the sobriety I found in AA, to own up to my faults and make amends to those I harmed, and to improve my conscious contact with God through prayer and meditation. Over time, I began to reach out to other alcoholics and pass along what I had been given—strength, hope and experience—to help them recover from alcoholism.

I believe that I am sober by the grace of God, and by God's grace alone. Over the years, I have seen God lift many others out of alcoholism and lead them to new life. I am no stranger to miracles.

In the quiet of the night, I wonder about Lazarus. Did he celebrate the mystery of his new life even when he took out the garbage on a cold, rainy night, feeling God's grace even then? I hope so, because I am, in a sense, Lazarus. I tasted death in alcoholism, and God has given me a glimpse of the resurrection.

—Tom, an alcoholic

Saint Maximilian Kolbe
patron of people with drug addiction

WHEN THE NAZIS INVADED POLAND IN SEPTEMBER OF 1939, the Franciscan friary where Maximilian lived sheltered and fed thousands of people, mostly Jews, who were trying to flee Poland. Maximilian, editor of a popular Catholic magazine, "The Knight," wrote against the Nazis. Soon after, the Nazis took him prisoner and sent him to the concentration camp at Auschwitz. In the horrible conditions of the camp, where starving prisoners were worked to total exhaustion, Maximilian determined to be a source of hope and love to the other prisoners. At risk to his life, he led them in prayer, gave spiritual conferences and heard their confessions.

One night a prisoner escaped. In retaliation, the commander randomly selected ten other prisoners from the same cell block to be executed. When one of these men begged for his life because he had a wife and children, Maximilian stepped forward to offer his own life instead. With the other nine prisoners he was sent to an underground bunker and left to starve to death. Two weeks later, the Nazis discovered that Maximilian was still alive. He was given a lethal injection on August 14, 1941.

After Maximilian's death, word spread through the camp about his selfless act of love. When Pope John Paul II canonized him in 1982 as a "martyr of charity," he named him the special patron of all those who struggle with drug addiction.

Saint Maximilian Kolbe's feast is August 14.

Pushing the chapel door open at six o'clock to go out for a morning walk by the river, I heard the familiar siren sounds. Not until my return did I find out that a man had been stabbed at our door. It was another drug deal gone wrong. That morning I had walked through Wallace's blood and did not know it.

At the Downtown Chapel in Portland, Oregon, the staff and numerous volunteers receive the homeless, the mentally ill, the drug-addicted and those in recovery into our Hospitality Center. Here they can come in out of the rainy cold, share hot coffee, receive clean clothes and share street stories. "Sam," an addict for thirty years, said he thought drugs would enable him to escape his loneliness but instead have caged him in isolation and destroyed every relationship he has ever had. "Adam" says he started drugs when he was seventeen. He immediately became homeless and tried prostitution for a while. He still goes on binges where he is awake for five days straight, and then crashes in unknown places and wakes up with strangers. Adam says being addicted is like having barbed wire around his heart and each hit tightens the grip.

Two weeks after Wallace's death, we gathered on the street where he was stabbed to claim our sidewalk and chapel entry in God's peace. I listened to people's stories of their friend Wallace. We cannot take the struggles away, but I am learning that our stories are all we have and telling them can help to lead us out of our addictions. As someone told me after the service, "These are the modern-day parables, the gospel to sink our teeth into." Addiction strangled life out of Wallace, but hope prevails when we pray on story-stained sidewalks.

—Ronald Raab, CSC

Saint Monica
patron of parents of troubled children

MONICA LIVED IN NORTH AFRICA IN THE FOURTH CENTURY, when Christians and pagans intermingled. She was a Christian and her husband, Patricius, a pagan. It was a difficult marriage and both drank too much. One day, one of their servants taunted Monica about her drinking, and she never drank again.

One of their sons, Augustine, would become one of the most famous men in the history of Christianity, but for a long time he was also her biggest worry. Augustine was a brilliant scholar but his way of life was far removed from Christian ideals. For many years, he stole, lied and had a mistress with whom he fathered a child.

Realizing that she alone could not make Augustine change his ways, Monica prayed to God for seventeen years for his conversion. One story says that people ran the other way— even the priest—when they saw her coming because of her constant requests for prayers for her wayward son.

When Augustine left North Africa and fled to Rome without telling her, she followed him. In Italy he met Ambrose, the bishop of Milan, and Augustine was on his way to becoming one of the greatest Christian theologians.

Monica was present at his baptism and asked Ambrose to be her own spiritual director. In the end, Monica and Augustine became very good friends and Augustine wrote of his grief when his mother died.

In this drawing, Monica, with rosary and tissues in her pocket, is presented as the mother of a teen who is being arrested. The blue lights of a police car highlight her sorrow. Parents know better than anyone all the dreams and potential that lie beneath their children's problems. Monica's persistent hope for her son is seen in parents of every age and culture.

Saint Monica's feast is August 27.

When I was growing up in the 1950s, some of my favorite TV programs were "Ozzie and Harriet," "Leave It to Beaver" and "Father Knows Best." The parents on these TV shows "problem-solved" so wisely and easily. Now I am a parent, and the wisdom of the old TV families just doesn't cut it.

As I wrestle with the problems my child has had, I have felt great fear, discouragement and hopelessness. I realize that in some ways I too have been a prodigal, not just my son.

In the end, I had to realize my own limitations and turn to my father in heaven, who truly knows best. When in my anguish I begged God for patience and the ability to be long-suffering, I heard God say to me, "I am long-suffering."

I have had to learn to trust God and to entrust my child to his care and his time and to wait and pray. This is a hard lesson for a parent. In my own suffering for my child, I have prayed two scripture texts over and over (perhaps two that Saint Monica also prayed): "Why so downcast? O my soul, put your hope in the Lord" and "Rejoice in hope, endure in affliction, persevere in prayer."

—*Philip Russell*

Saint Peregrine
patron of people with cancer

PEREGRINE ONCE SLAPPED SAINT PHILIP BENIZI IN THE FACE just because he didn't like his message. In deep remorse over what he had done, he had a conversion of heart and became a devoted Christian. He joined a religious order, the Servites, in Siena, Italy, after Mary instructed him to do so in a vision. He came to be called the "Angel of Good Counsel" because of his loving manner with the poor and the sick, to whom he dispensed good advice and healing.

When he was sixty years old, Peregrine developed a painful and repulsive cancer of the foot and leg. He suffered with it for years before it was decided that the leg should be amputated. The night before surgery, Peregrine prayed fervently before his favorite crucifix. In yet another life-changing vision, Christ came off the cross and healed his cancer. Peregrine lived until he was eighty without a trace of cancer.

Jesus on the cross keeps watch with Peregrine as he undergoes his chemotherapy treatment. Peregrine is a good companion for all those living with cancer and the many anxieties that come with it. His life of service and compassion shed beautiful light on Christ's words in the border: Do not worry about tomorrow.

Saint Peregrine's feast is May 1.

For as long as I can remember, I was driven to make it on my own. By my mid-twenties, I had put myself through college, had a well-paying, fast-track job, and was married to a wonderful wife. I was in control. Then I noticed a lump near my left hip. Even as the nurses were preparing me for surgery to remove the lump, I was confident that nothing bad could happen to me—I was in control. When my doctor telephoned me and said the word cancer—I was stunned. How could this be? I didn't feel sick at all, and I thought I was much too young to have such a serious illness. This was not part of my plan. At first I felt numb, then angry, then defeated and terrified.

A few days after my diagnosis, a large group of family members and friends gathered together to pray for me. Each person laid hands on me and made the sign of the cross on my forehead. The love, support and humor of the people in my faith community gave me strength, determination and hope for the struggle that lay ahead of me. I quickly realized that this was not a battle I could face alone. Thankfully, I did not have to. The treatment was difficult and made me feel physically weak, but the support I received made me stronger and gave me courage to face each challenge that arose as the months of treatment wore on.

Today I have been cancer-free for almost three years. I can see now, even more than I did then, that from this challenge, many positive things emerged. It affirmed to me the power of community, and made me feel very much that we are not alone. It deepened my sense of faith. This journey has helped me to understand that some things are beyond my control and do not always go as I plan. But even in times of great fear, when people gather in God's name, anything is possible.

—Anthony J. Krolak

Saint Rita
patron of people in difficult marriages

RITA WAS MARRIED VERY YOUNG TO A CRUEL MAN, PAOLO, who was involved in street violence and crime. During their eighteen years of marriage, he beat her, was unfaithful and neglected her and their twin sons. At that time, in the eyes of the law and the church, she had no right to leave him, and no means of supporting herself and her children if she did. Paolo was murdered in a vendetta and his body was left on Rita's doorstep. When their sons vowed revenge, Rita prayed that they would die rather than commit murder. They became ill and shortly before their deaths, they declared their forgiveness of their father's killers.

Finally free after all those years of desperate turmoil and family obligations, Rita entered the Augustinian convent where she spent the rest of her long life.

It is autumn in this drawing of Saint Rita, a time in the north when summer dies in a blaze of glory and we are reminded of the necessity of death. Surrounding her head is a thorny vine, recalling a vision she had in which a thorn from Christ's crown of thorns pierced her forehead. Meditating on nature is one of the best, most direct ways to pray. Perhaps two leaves have inspired Saint Rita to reflect on the events of her painful life with her husband, and the death that winter brings. But bountiful life will return in spring.

Saint Rita's feast is August 27.

Growing up in a home where love was unconditional and fairly balanced, I was unprepared for a marriage where love became a volley for control. In trying so hard to be reasonable, I lost all ability to reason. Only someone who has experienced the chaos of physical, emotional, spiritual or verbal abuse at the hands of someone who claims to love her, or someone with extraordinary empathy can comprehend the quicksand that surrounds a troubled or violent marriage.

And it is a quicksand that threatens to swallow its victims whole. Not only at times did I feel there was no rope to pull me out, I hadn't told any family or friends I needed one. Knowing there is support is the only way someone can extricate herself from the suffocation of the soul that accompanies an abusive marriage. The knowledge that someone will understand and offer concrete assistance in a non-judgmental way is freeing and energizing.

I closed my eyes to the reality that my life was not as it seemed. I completely and fully understand how my wishes for a fulfilling, content marriage made me lie to myself and to the world. I completely understand how and why my dreams made me blind.

But true joy comes from seeing the world not as I wished it to be in a fantasy. True joy comes from telling myself the truth and making amends to create a life that is peaceful. The truth is a gift that is a solid structure upon which we can build new dreams.

—Michelle Weldon

Saint Teresa of Avila
patron of people with headaches

TERESA OF AVILA IS ONE OF THE MOST ASTONISHING WOMEN in history—in or out of the church. She was the first woman to be declared a Doctor of the Church because she wrote some of the greatest spiritual books—at a time when women often couldn't read even the Bible! She was one of the key leaders of the Catholic Counter-Reformation who challenged—and was challenged by—church leaders for her new and daring thoughts. She was a keen businesswoman and administrator who founded an order and personally opened seventeen monasteries throughout Spain. And, in the midst of it all, she had two consistent companions: a terrific sense of humor and terrible headaches.

Teresa was beautiful, charming, witty and highly intelligent. When she was 39, she realized that she desired a more spiritual life and sought permission to form a new community dedicated to prayer, silence and fasting.

This drawing is filled with enough details to give any saint a headache! The castle on the left refers to her great book, *The Interior Castle*. Notes and memos around the office and in the border bear some of her writings and point to the endless energy and activity that filled Teresa's life—including lunch with her best friend, Saint John of the Cross. The quill pen in her pencil holder reminds us that she is a Doctor of the Church. And the pair of shoes atop her printer recalls that the nuns of her new order, the Discalced Carmelites, didn't wear shoes. The quotation in the border was Teresa's response to God after she was thrown from her carriage into the mud.

The bottles of aspirin and aromatherapy spray (she loved perfume) might be modern headache remedies, but Teresa maintained that silence and solitude are the best remedies for all ailments because they help us to discover the patient endurance that attains all things—especially the love of God.

Saint Teresa of Avila's feast is October 15.

It has never been clear to me why suffering would be more precious to God than heartfelt joy or honest pleasure. I was, therefore, a uniquely unsuitable candidate for the affliction of ghastly headaches that followed a ten-hour neurosurgery several years ago. Surgery went well, but I found myself with what I could only describe as "railroad spike headaches" that began as neck stiffness and progressed in minutes to intense pain behind my right ear, often involving my forehead and face. As a marathon runner and kayaker, a high-energy woman used to sleeping little and juggling much, I found it frankly humiliating to stop and curl up as quickly as possible. Even the word "headache" was unwelcome. This crushing pain was unlike anything I had ever known . . . and there was nothing I could do but wait. I am at home with words and reasoning, but I had neither the will nor the energy for either in the presence of this pain. Nor could I pray, at least not as I knew, in prayer of grateful friendship in the presence of God. Even protestation was beyond me. And thus, time after unwelcome time, I waited in the darkness for sleep to come, able only to listen to the sound of my own heart, my own breathing. These days the headaches come far less often and are diminished enough in intensity that I can keep working and talking and thinking. I am grateful for this. But I also know that each of us will come to a time in which all our words and earnest effort and prayer itself will fall away. Even our simple breathing and beating heart will fail. What will remain is the gift that was always there: the radically simple and undeserved love beyond our comprehension, present in death as in life, in pain as in joy.

—*Jill Joseph*

Saint Timothy
patron of people with stomach ailments

TIMOTHY, A YOUTHFUL STUDENT AND COMPANION OF SAINT Paul, converted to Christianity during a time of persecution. Perhaps such stressful times brought him ulcers, because in Paul's famous First Letter to Timothy, Paul suggests that he take a little wine for his stomach and all his other ailments.

Timothy is on board a boat because Paul, who thought of him as a son, chose him to be a traveling preacher to such far-flung places as Corinth, Thessalonica and Galatia.

Paul wrote two letters, now part of the New Testament, to Timothy in Ephesus with instructions on how to be a good bishop and deacon. In the second letter Saint Paul speaks of the timeless Christian virtues of resolve, patience, love and endurance—all good qualities to have—with or without an upset stomach!

Saint Timothy's feast is January 26.

Until I was invited to write this essay, I didn't realize that Timothy was the patron of people with stomach trouble. Oddly, I grew up in a parish dedicated to Saint Timothy but the story of this particular area of his influence never surfaced. I do, however, know about prayers being offered on behalf of someone with stomach disease.

Almost three years ago I was diagnosed with a malignant tumor in my stomach. It was detected very early and it was small—about the size of a dime—but its location required the removal of my whole stomach. On the day of the surgery, my parishioners decided to hold a prayer vigil. I joined them at 6 a.m., just before leaving for the hospital, and when I entered the church I found that every icon we own—together with a fair number that people had brought from home—was on display, surrounded by a blaze of candles and with flowers banking the statue of Our Lady. The vigil continued until the congregation had been informed that I was awake in the recovery room, some eight hours later.

Virtually every member of the parish came to the church that day, spent time in prayer and turned their thoughts to their priest "with stomach trouble." Since then, prayer vigils have become the norm at Grace Church. We hold them when people are in surgery, when we know that someone among us is dying, when airplanes are crashing into skyscrapers in New York. I don't know if people in prayer at these vigils invoke the name of Timothy. Who knows? Some may. But I do know that our people feel profoundly connected to one another when they turn their thoughts to God in times of trouble. And I certainly felt profoundly connected to them as they prayed for me.

—Reverend Michael Johnston

Saint Vincent de Paul
patron of elderly people

THE NAME OF VINCENT DE PAUL IS SYNONYMOUS WITH THE virtue of charity. He expressed his deep lifelong love for suffering humanity in a variety of ways: He gathered homeless and abandoned children from the streets of Paris and placed them in orphanages. He founded hospitals for the sick and poor who had nowhere else to turn. He visited prisoners and comforted slaves as they waited to be shipped abroad. To help him in this work he founded a religious community for men named the Congregation of the Mission, often called the Vincentians, and another for women, the Daughters or Sisters of Charity.

Vincent had entered the diocesan seminary because he saw ordination as a way out of poverty. He did become chaplain to the queen of France and other people of the court, but his heart led him back to his first and longest lasting love, the poor.

Despite a lifetime of various illnesses and pains, including asthma, stomach trouble, and leg ulcers, Saint Vincent lived to the age of 80. He rode his horse until he was 69, and even when his health deteriorated, he still rose before dawn to pray and keep up with his enormous correspondence. In his last years, as his sight and strength failed, Saint Vincent needed a cane to walk. Eventually, he had to be carried to the chapel for daily Mass.

Since Saint Vincent de Paul is usually depicted with children, he is shown here celebrating his birthday with a little boy. Behind them is a birthday card from his good friend, Saint Louise de Marillac, with whom he founded the order of sisters. By the time of his death, Saint Vincent de Paul had gained the renown he had desired as a youth. But it came for reasons he never would have dreamed of—he was known for his enormously loving heart.

Saint Vincent de Paul's feast is September 27.

I work as a physician taking care of older people; I specialize in internal medicine with added qualifications in geriatrics. My work allows me to assist older people in maintaining their health and independence, as well as to care for people when their health fails and they face some of the difficulties of aging.

I decided to focus on geriatrics because I like older people. The gifts of aging often include an honesty about life, a generosity in caring and a thankfulness for the good things life has brought. When I am with many of my patients it reminds me of a beautiful day in autumn: the warmth of summer remains in the air but there is a brilliance of color in the trees because the season is changing. Likewise, older people bring a vitality and brilliance to life, even as life changes from the experience of youth and middle age.

Taking care of older people can also be sad. It means accompanying people in difficult times, when illness may take away a person's ability to function independently or signal a decline that will result in death. Medicine cannot fix everything. Sometimes the best I can do is work to limit suffering and make sure my patients know that they are not alone.

Some of the last stages of life, however, are the most rewarding for me as a physician. To be a trusted companion to my patients as they are dying makes me feel honored. When I can ease pain and discomfort by the skillful use of medications and with the help of other caring people like nurses, therapists and aides, I am proud to be a physician. As my patients move from this life to the next, I thank God for their lives and for God's presence in my work.

—*Myles N. Sheehan,* SJ, MD

about the contributors

Ann M. Bergart, a clinical social worker in the Chicago area for more than thirty years and a professor of social work, struggled with infertility for over seven years. She is a leader and member of the board of directors for RESOLVE, an organization devoted to education, support and advocacy for infertile couples.

Patricia Bolin lives in a Chicago suburb with her son, Tim. She enjoys cooking, baking and reading, and volunteers for Misericordia, a home for developmentally delayed children and adults. Her daughters, Meghan, Sara and Colleen, all are recently married. The family is grieving the sudden death of another son, Kevin, in an auto accident.

Antoinette Bosco is a syndicated columnist for Catholic News Service and the author of nine books. Her most recent book, *Choosing Mercy: A Mother of Murder Victims Pleads to End the Death Penalty,* received a 2001 Christopher Award. She is the mother of seven children, two of whom are deceased, and has developed a bereavement ministry for those suffering the loss of a loved one.

Kathy Brown is the Advocacy Manager in Church Outreach at Catholic Relief Services. Before coming to CRS, Kathy served as the dean of theological studies for the Diocese of Phoenix, Arizona, diocesan director of the Office of Peace and Justice, and director of institutes for The North American Forum on the Catechumenate. She has worked for the church for over 25 years. Her areas of expertise are social justice, catechetics, initiation and liturgy.

Melissa Collingwood has lived in Los Gatos, California, for 20 years, working with several Silicon Valley high-tech firms. She is a collector of collage art and is working toward a career in graphic design and production.

Thomas J. Como is a social worker and psychotherapist. He has worked with the chronically mentally ill in hospitals and institutions, and currently has a private practice specializing in relationship and adjustment issues.

Jacqueline (Jacqui) Bernadette Coppola is 11 years old and in fifth grade at Saint Andrew School, Newtown, Pennsylvania. She enjoys watching sports on TV, especially football and basketball, and playing basketball and swimming. She also likes to draw and color, just like her uncle, the author and artist of *Patrons and Protectors.*

Christopher de Vinck is a high school teacher and administrator in New Jersey. His writings on family, education and children and his poetry have been published in the *New York Times,* the *Wall Street Journal,* the *National Catholic Reporter, Catholic Digest, America* and *Poetry Review.* His book, *The Power of the Powerless,* is the story of his brother, Oliver.

Sarah Doherty is a Chicago native currently studying history and international affairs at Xavier University in Cincinnati. She spent a semester living and working in Kathmandu, Nepal, to better understand the struggles one faces growing up in a developing nation.

Elizabeth Fox is retired after teaching elementary school for 36 years. She does some substitute teaching and is a volunteer at Ronald McDonald Children's Hospital at Loyola University Medical Center.

Margaret Harte is a breast cancer survivor and the founder of the annual Mother's Day Walk for the Cure held in Chicago's Grant Park.

William (Bill) Hocker, a psychotherapist, is studying at the Church Divinity School of the Pacific, a seminary of the Episcopal church. His service focuses on work at the food pantry of his parish, Saint Gregory of Nyssa, in San Francisco.

Anita Houck is assistant professor of religious studies at Saint Mary's College, Notre Dame, Indiana. A former high-school teacher and parish pastoral associate, she's received degrees from Wesleyan University, Harvard Graduate School of Education and the University of Chicago Divinity School.

Michael Johnston is an Episcopal priest and the pastor of Grace Church, Oak Park, Illinois. A New Testament scholar and art historian, he is the author of *Engaging the Word,* a book on holy scripture for the laity. He brings to his teaching and preaching a unique understanding of Christian history, theology and spirituality as revealed by the art and architecture of the church. He is at work on a new book, *Engaging the Image*.

Thomas J. Johnston is a member of the Order of Preachers working in the Office of the Dominican Shrine of Saint Jude Thaddeus, 1909 South Ashland Avenue, Chicago IL 60608-2994.

Jill Joseph, MD, is a public health scientist and a pediatrician who works in Washington. She is the director of a center that works to improve children's health.

Anthony J. Krolak lives in the Chicago area. He keeps himself busy as the director of national operations and development for a rapidly growing company. His interests are varied, including playing guitar, astronomy, hiking and camping.

Lillian Lewis is a psychotherapist in private practice and a spiritual director. She also directs the religious education program in her church community.

Marlena McCarthy has been a flight attendant for over 30 years. She lives in Oak Park, Illinois.

Lynne Marie Meyer is an adult survivor of childhood sexual abuse. In addition to a master's degree in Jewish studies earned at Chicago's Spertus Institute, she holds a master of theological studies degree in world religions from the Divinity School of Harvard University. Lynne is currently the executive secretary for the Illinois conference of the American Association of University Professors.

Jamie O'Reilly has been a vital contributor to Chicago's rich cultural landscape for over 20 years. She is a producer, award winning playwright, and a multifaceted performer with a vibrant, soulful connection to her audience and her repertoire.

Susan Carew Perez is the director of Tolton Adult Education Center in Chicago, which offers classes in adult and family literacy as well as workplace skills. She has served in education for over 35 years.

Ronald Raab, CSC, is a Holy Cross priest serving at St. Vincent Parish's Downtown Chapel in Portland, Oregon. He also preaches retreats and parish missions around the country.

Philip Russell is a hairdresser and salon owner in Virginia. He and his wife recently received a call from their son, who said, "I'm sorry. I love you both."

Myles Sheehan, SJ, MD, is a Jesuit priest and physician who practices at Loyola University Medical Center in Maywood, Illinois. He is senior associate dean of the education program at Loyola's Stritch School of Medicine where he teaches medical students about aging, ethics and end of life care.

Maryrose Smith is a licensed clinical social worker. Her vision is improving and her life is returning to a new normal.

Tom is a partner in a Chicago-based company that offers legal technology consulting to law firms and law departments nation-wide. Tom ministers to alcoholics and is an RCIA catechist at his parish. His last name is withheld because AA members remain anonymous when discussing AA in public.

Michelle Weldon is an author, journalist and popular speaker. She was featured on Oprah Winfrey's television program to discuss her book, *Writing to Save Your Life: How to Honor Your Life,* for which she won the Chicago Women in Publishing 2002 Excellence Award. Her first book, *I Closed My Eyes,* has been translated into five languages. She is a senior lecturer at Northwestern University's Medill School of Journalism.

about the artist

Brother Michael (Mickey) O'Neill McGrath, OSFS, is an
Oblate of Saint Francis de Sales in Washington, D.C.,
whose full-time ministry is art. In addition to creating art
for most of today's leading Catholic publishers as well as
parishes nationwide, Mickey conducts retreats, workshops
and parish missions centered on the relationship between
art, prayer and religious faith.